WORD WARPS:

A glossary of unfamiliar terms

Written and illustrated by
DAVID DIEFENDORF

MULLER, BLOND & WHITE

The author would like to thank **The New York Times,**
The Village Voice and **The San Francisco Chronicle** for permission
to reprint selected items appearing in this book.

First published in Great Britain in 1986 by
Muller, Blond & White Limited,
55 Great Ormond Street, London WC1N 3HZ,
by arrangement with Williamson Publishing, Vermont.

British Library Cataloguing in Publication Data

Diefendorf, David.
Word warps: a glossary of unfamiliar terms.
1. English language — dictionaries.
I. Title.
423′.1   PE1628
ISBN 0 584 11147–9

Printed and bound in Great Britain by
R. J. Acford, Chichester, Sussex.

Love and thanks to Esther, Bill, Beth,
Glenn, Ellen, Barbara, Stu, Ferris,
Jack, Susan, Ken, and Karen.
_____

OCTOPUS:

a cat with only 8 lives

JEJUNE:

the month after Memay and before Jejuly

POLYPHONY:

---

a versatile impostor

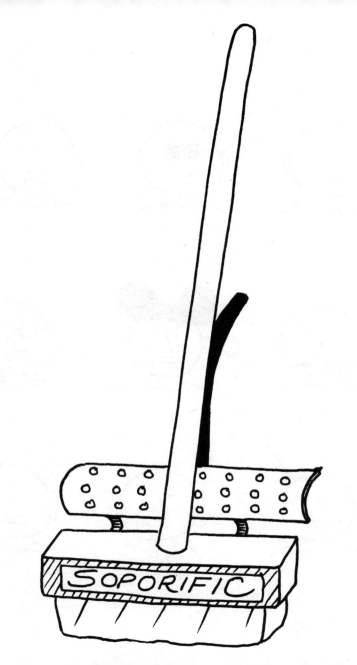

SOPORIFIC:

a new miracle mop

CYCLAMATES:

a gang of bikers

MENU
PARCHEESI OFFERINGS
(our specialty!)

Parcheesi Omelette 2.95
Parcheesi Danish 1.50
Parcheesi Veal 6.95
Parcheesi Broccoli 4.75
Parcheesi Crackers 75
Parcheesi Cake 2.00
Macaroni Parcheesi 3.08
Parcheesi du jour 5.99
Parcheesi U-name-it . . . . ?

PARCHEESI:

containing cheese and other ingredients

OLFACTORY:

a building that now contains expensive lofts

LISTLESS:

having to grocery-shop from memory

RAGTIME:

the time when an article of clothing is no longer fit to wear

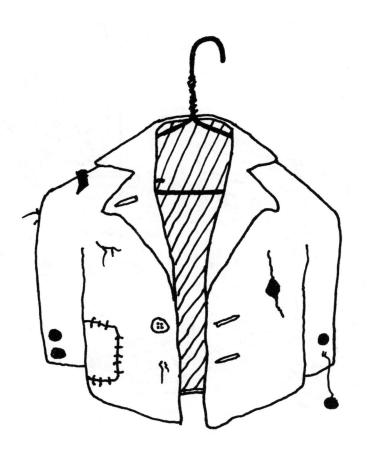

RAISON D'ETRE:

a French breakfast cereal

BOMBARD:

a poet who reads very badly

DILATE:

to phone someone after 11 PM

PECCADILLO:

a relative of the armadillo

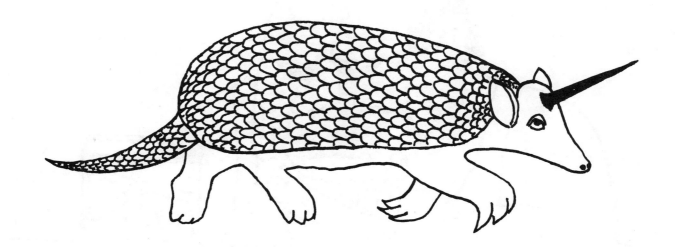

HEBREW:

a beer for men only

SALMONELLA:

rags-to-riches fairy tale about a young fisherwoman

PORTUGUESE:

the plural of Portugoose

COUNTERCULTURE:

life at a diner

ESCHEW:

Spanish gum

BRAHMAN:

transvestite

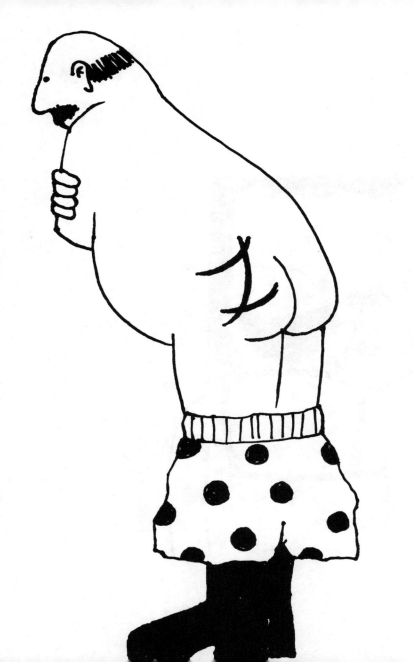

ZOROASTRIAN:

one who bears the mark of Zoro

CANTALOUPE:

to be unable to run off with a lover

EGALITARIAN:

eagle-worshipper

STUCCO:

past tense of "sticco"

Fig. 1

Fig. 2

BLUNDERBUSS:

an awkwardly placed kiss

CATACOMB:

grooming tool for cats

HIPPOCAMPUS:

a college that attracts fat people

TURNCOAT:

a reversible jacket

Fig. 1

Fig. 2

CRUSTACEAN:

an aficionado of stale bread

DUCKWEED:

a plant that quacks

CASTANET:

command shouted by fishermen

SMOTHER:

an overprotective mother

DEBARK:

what protects detree

DETREE

DEBARK

WINDBREAKER:

one who has a reputation for flatulence

SUMMERSAULT:

sault that will pour in humid weather

SUMMER
SAULT

POURS IN HOT, STICKY
WEATHER — OR RAIN

WARNING: WILL NOT
POUR IN WINTER

RESTITUTION:

a place where nervous people go to relax

MANDRAKE:

a creature half man, half duck

XENOPHOBIA:

fear of a Xen master

HICCUP:

cup used in the deep country

DIFFIDENT:

not the same

MACCABEES:

Scottish honey-gathering insects

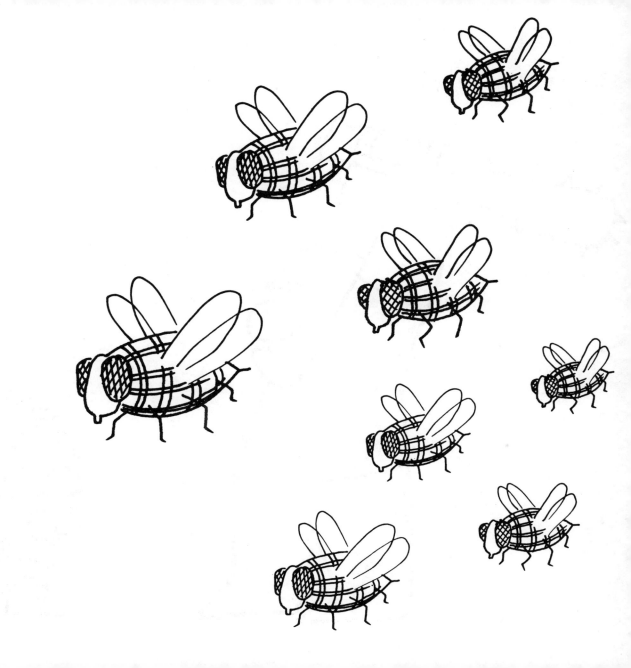

BUSHWHACKER:

one who is unkind to shrubs

CYCLONE:

an exact replica of someone named Cy

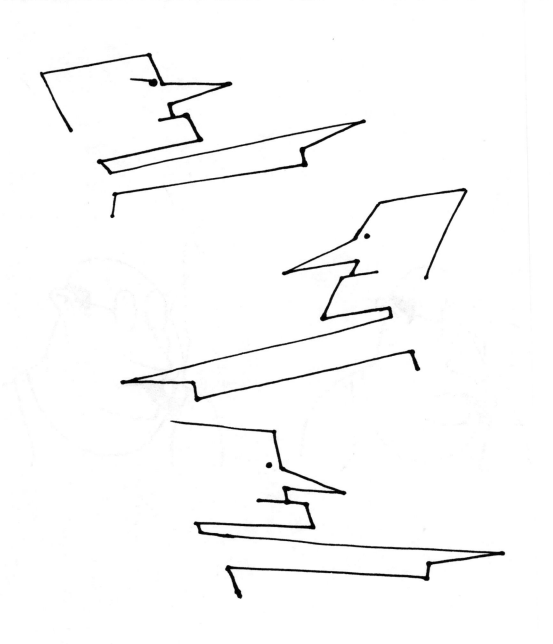

ACUMEN:

men noted for their precision

PRECURSOR:

one who has not yet learned to swear

MARIONETTE:

a very small bride

LIABILITY:

the ability to lie well

SELF-ESTEEM:

what comes out of your mouth on a cold day

GRUESOME:

is slightly taller

OXYMORON:

an especially stupid ox

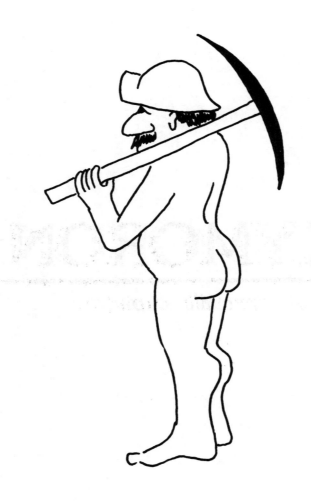

STRIP MINER:

a miner who likes to work in the nude

ENDORSE:

not outside

GRUEL:

very unkind

PALETTE:

a small friend

DOGMATIC:

a dog that cleans up its own mess

SCHERZO:

the Marx brother who terrified children

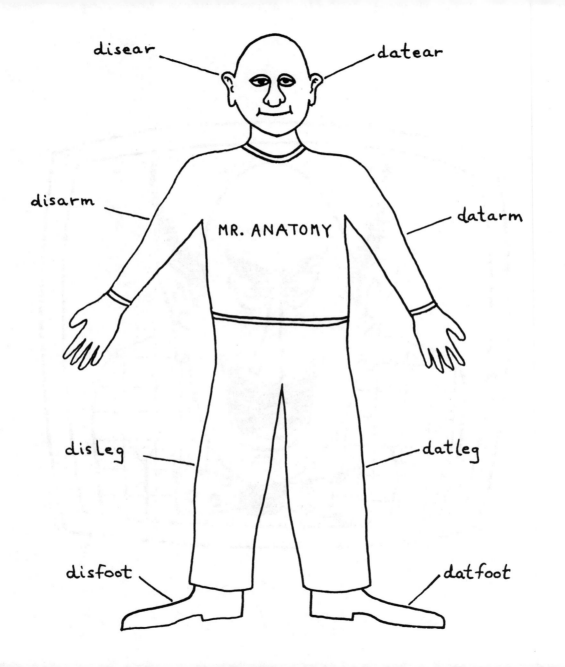

DISARM:

opposite of datarm

LECITHIN:

fatter

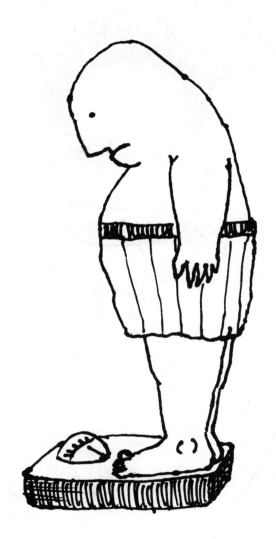

HOG-TIE:

a necktie having unsightly food stains

MALEMUTE:

a quiet person who thinks bad thoughts

MAHATMA:

the utterance of a confused person looking for his hat

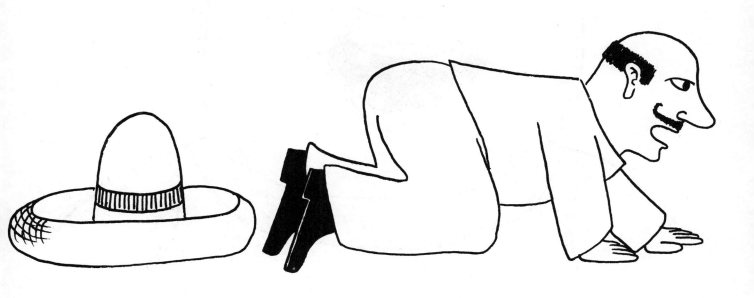

DECADENT:

someone having exactly ten teeth

PARASITE:

someone who lives in Paras

UNDERDOG:

the most unpleasant part of a dog's body